EASTERN SHORE BECKONINGS

by John Pearson

To Ann & Herald
John Pearson

Recovery Communications, Inc.
P.O. Box 19910 • Baltimore, MD 21211 • (410) 243-8558

Acknowledgements

Without the support of family, friends and other writers this book would not have been written.

My sisters helped me remember things. My writing group taught me to write. Nan Yarnall supported me when the need was greatest. My childhood friend Joe Valliant aided me throughout the procedure.

My old friend Peggy Fox took the picture which appears on the back cover.

Lastly, I thank my publisher and editor Toby Rice Drews for her work and enthusiasm.

CHAPTER ONE

In 1948 my parents took possession of a small furnished house and land at Jack's Point, outside of Oxford on Maryland's Eastern Shore. The previous owner, a widower, had only taken some clothes and a revolver that hung in its holster from the bedside table in the master bedroom. Everything else was left: photographs, yearbooks, sewing boxes. All the necessary and accumulated things.

My mother never said, but somehow communicated, to me that it was reprehensible of the widower to leave all of his late wife's things, keeping nothing, not even a photograph. My mother put some of these things away as if she were saving them for somebody.

The house, white clapboard surrounded by screened porches, had rooms dark and musty, heated by fireplaces in the winter. There were two outbuildings. A one room cabin which became mine.

My mother found the services of a stout and good-natured black woman and the two of them began to clean the house and outbuildings.

I was put in charge of picking through and deciding what would be thrown out and what saved. Old Naval officer's uniforms, *Life* magazines from the Second World War, license tags for cars from the 1920's, old duck decoys, muskrat traps, old rusty shotguns, and hipboots with holes in them.

CHAPTER TWO

One summer night, I was in my tree by the river. It must have been a Saturday night, and across the creek the Musgraves were having their usual argument.

Mr. Musgrave, known as "Muskrat", was drunk. Mrs. Musgrave was yelling at him, their voices carrying well over the water. He threatened to push her off the pier.

"You can't push me while I'm a holdin this here babah," she shouted.

"You just wait and see," was his reply. With that he gave her a shove, adroitly grabbing the baby out of her arms. She hit the water with a loud splash. The baby never made a sound.

After some shouting and splashing, "Muskrat" helped his wife back onto the pier. I never heard them argue outside the house again.

CHAPTER THREE

I wasn't much of a hand in the garden and my mother's plans were too grand for her own energy to accomplish, so another hired hand was found in the person of Dave. Dave was, I guess, around sixty at the time and was a tall, lanky, tobacco-chewing black man. He was put in charge of gardening and I was to help him.

Dave first cut out the edges of the garden and then with a hand plough turned the soil. That done, we mixed in fertilizer and peat moss with the turned earth. This was hard work and in the sun of the Eastern Shore summer sweat ran off both of us. Little was said the first week Dave was on the job, but I could easily tell that he was good-natured and had a sense of humor.

As the season wore on the work became lighter and Dave and I began to talk more. He had a raft of stories and enjoyed telling them.

My mother caught us one day leaning on our hoes talking and laughing. She asked Dave what had been done that day. He replied in accents that I couldn't understand with tobacco juice running down his chin while he mumbled. My mother went back to the house shaking her head.

I said to Dave, "I always understand everything you say, but while you were talking to my mother I didn't get a word."

"Yeah," he said, "When white folks gets too bossy you got

to put the code on um." That incident seemed to break the ice between us, and Dave began to talk more about his life and ideas.

Some days later Dave and I were in the back garden when he began a story. "Black folks is mighty superstitious. We get real nervous at funerals. Some time back I took ventriloquism lessons. I never got real good but if no one was looking at me hard I could make a voice come out of another place or person.

"Well, we was all at a funeral of an old friend of mine. All the pallbearers were lowering the box down into the hole. I threw my voice into the coffin and said. 'Lower me down easy boys.' Well, they hollered and scattered in all directions."

ᘓ

Most of the time Dave's stories were less far-fetched. In those days, I liked anything to do with war and I got Dave to tell me about his experiences in the Great War. He said that he had seen no action or Germans. Throughout the year he was in France he never left Le Havre where he and other "Negro" soldiers unloaded ships.

"I sure did like France though. Colored folks didn't get treated the same way they be treated here. No Sir, they wasn't any separate outhouses, or restaurants, or separate anything. Colored folks could go anywhere. We had trouble sometimes with the white soldiers, but never with the Frenchies."

"How did you feel about coming home again?"

"I didn't have no choice in the matter. They just put us on a ship one day and home we sailed. The next thing I knew I was back down here on the shore."

I had been brought up by a black woman and had heard many things from her viewpoint but I had never before heard things that so clearly bespoke the black experience in a white world.

At the time I just took Dave's stories in. But as I thought about what he had told me I felt let into his world.

CHAPTER FOUR

My mother spoke fondly of Olivia, the late wife of the previous owner of Jack's Point. It was as if they had known one another, or, at least, as if mother had known her.

On rainy days I would pore through Olivia's old boarding school and college yearbooks. I found her portrait photograph as a senior in the Vassar class of 1928. Her head was tilted to the right and her pale blond hair was spot lit. She had a long face with large pale eyes. Her lips were full and cheekbones high. The hair style, severe.

Again when these books were opened that musty smell came back. Smell has always been a trigger of memory for me.

☙

I was in my bedroom cabin lying on my bed reading a magazine and I could see, through the open door, my mother on her knees by an ivy patch surrounding a large cherry tree which stood at the back of the main house. Her lips were moving as she dug with a trowel. She was talking and talking as she worked. I had never seen her do this before so I asked her later, "Who were you talking to while you were working in the ivy today?"

"Olivia. I often talk to her. When I tell her what worries me I always feel better afterward."

I didn't doubt Mother's words. I had found out that I could communicate with imagined persons. As a child I had had what adults call "an imaginary friend", and we had talked together for hours when I was supposedly playing alone on the hillside behind our Baltimore house. So it wasn't much of a stretch for me to believe that my mother could converse with the ghost of Olivia.

Soon the main house and the outbuildings were cleaned, stripped of unwanted things, and painted. Now my mother's real work could begin, the gardening and the "putting up" of the garden's produce. Tomatoes, corn, beans, pickled watermelon rind.

CHAPTER FIVE

I would ask anyone we met if they had any antique weapons — old guns or swords.

The next house up the dirt road belonged to an ancient couple named Butler. Mr. Butler was an invalid looked after by his wife. I knew in my bones that the Butler house was loaded with treasure, and I resolved to get into the good graces of the Butlers.

I can't remember how I did it but one day I was sitting next to Mr. Butler in their living room. I asked him about guns. We had found something in common. He wheeled himself over to a tall chest of drawers across the room. He came back with several pistols. I was in heaven.

One was a Civil War Colt Navy model and the other was a very sinister-looking, First World War-vintage, German automatic. He had taken the German pistol from a prisoner during his service in the First World War. The Civil War revolver had been carried by an ancestor in that war.

My instincts were working; there were treasures in the Butler house. I went back several times more and talked with Mr. Butler in his hot parlor with the loud ticking clock and smell of coal oil. He was a lonely man and enjoyed having somebody to talk to. Mrs. Butler really never had much to say.

When Mr. Butler died, Mother and I called on Mrs. Butler with some food Mother had cooked for the occasion. After that, however, Mrs. Butler seemed to retreat. I seldom saw her outside of the house. Once in a while a daughter would visit her from out of town.

About a year later, Mrs. Butler died. The daughter came with a moving van and took everything away, including an ancient Hudson car which was always in the garage and never driven. The house was sold to another taciturn couple whom I remember nothing of.

CHAPTER SIX

Next to the Butlers lived the Hobbses. When we first arrived at Jack's Point Mrs. Hobbs came down the road to welcome us. She said at one point, "This your boy? I've got ten head of chilren myself." I couldn't believe my ears, "ten head of chilren". I'd heard of counting cattle by the head, but children? This was a new one. When I asked my mother about it later she said, "that is just country talk."

Mr. Hobbs was a waterman. Some might call him a fisherman, but he took his living from the water. The bay yields crabs in the summer and oysters in the winter, so waterman best covers the occupation.

Mr. Hobbs also kept a terrapin pen at the back of his yard at the edge of the creek. The Hobbses' backyard came right down to the creek, and across two thirds of it Mr. Hobbs had driven wide long boards into the ground and out into the bottom of the creek, forming a square of about eighteen feet. The greater part was fenced water. The boards in the water had turned almost black.

He had dumped sand on the land side for the terrapins to bury their eggs. Most of the time the terrapins were in the water, but occasionally I could see one or two crawling around in the sand pile.

Mr. Hobbs explained to me one day about his terrapin business. "I catch turipins while I'm oat tendin moy crab pots and add 'em to moy stock. Some of 'em breed and it expands that way too. Come winter a fellow come down from Balmer and I sell him as many as he'dan carry at a toyme."

ᘓ

Some mornings I'd wake up very early, just as the sun was rising. I'd look out the window of my cabin, the one that faced the creek. There would be Mr. Hobbs standing in the back of his skiff, sculling with one oar out to his work boat. He would quietly board and then start the single cycle engine and "put, put, put" out into the river.

The grace of Mr. Hobbs' rowing affected my mother as well; she once said, "Mr. Hobbs stands so straight and moves so gracefully he must have some Indian blood in him."

ᘓ

Mr. Hobbs was very fond of reading the Bible, so I asked him what religion he belonged to. He was a Seventh Day Adventist.

"What is that religion, Mr Hobbs?"

"Well, it's pretty much like other religions except the Sabbath is Saturday. That appealed to me because then I could take Saturday and Sunday off from working."

Little, wrinkled Mrs. Hobbs looked up from her sewing and smiled.

CHAPTER SEVEN

Across the road from the Hobbses lived a family from Connecticut. These were not country people. They had moved down to the Eastern Shore. Walter, their youngest child, and I became friends.

The Mayhews got a television. Sometimes on a Saturday night I would be invited to join the family to watch a show like "Lights Out", a mystery program.

My parents resisted getting a television. I had watched this wondrous box several other times back in Baltimore, but the Mayhews treated TV like a small in-house theater. A program was watched with everybody seated in a semi-circle in front of the screen in their living room. Sometimes Mrs. Mayhew would hand out freshly baked Toll House cookies.

I would return home after one of these evenings longing for a television of my own.

CHAPTER EIGHT

The beach club had a food and drink counter where cokes and hamburgers were available. This stand was run by a large blond-headed woman who made the best hamburgers I've tasted. She said that her secret was adding tomato juice to the meat.

Blondie also had folk wisdom. I told her I had noticed cotton stuffed in holes in the screen door of an Inn in the town. "If you stick cotton in a hole in your screen it will keep the flies out."

For years I believed that flies had an aversion to raw cotton.

CHAPTER NINE

On Oxford's Main Street a few businesses were
gathered around the firehouse, in the middle of that mostly
residential street. When we first arrived in Oxford, Mother
and I explored these shops. There was an IGA grocery store,
a confectionary store, and Miss Liza's.

Miss Liza was a widow lady who lived over, and behind,
her store. Her shop was in the front two rooms of a two-and-
a-half story frame house. Large panes of mullioned glass
made up the front windows which flanked the tall front door.
The windows were crammed with all sorts of things both old
and new. The shop sold whatever Miss Liza deemed
appropriate.

The window display changed only in part. A fixture was
a two-foot plaster cast sculpture of Martha Washington at her
spinning wheel, with George Washington standing by her
side. This was one of a series popular in the Victorian era.

There would be a stack of calico-covered lamp shades on
a pressed-glass oil lamp; stacks of print tablecloths and
napkins; and a pine cottage chest of drawers with an embroi-
dered cloth on top, with pewter candlesticks and an oval gilt
mirror over it. Sewing things of all kinds were arranged here
and there. A painted rocking chair would be draped with a
folded crocheted coverlet. A boxed airplane model would
peek out from behind a quilted tea-cozy.

The interior of the shop was dimly lit by shaded lamps and was yet darkened by a roofed sidewalk in front of the shop. The shop was always cool in the summer. The shaded interior plus a window fan at the back of the shop kept the air moving.

There was a small aisle up the middle of the shop's front room full of treasures. The back room was a work space for Miss Liza and was also used for storage of stock.

When Mother would visit the shop to pick up a gift or to buy a lamp shade, I would work my way behind the right-hand display window and look at the plaster cast of the Washingtons. The group had a low, glossy tan surface, which heightened the antique appearance of the piece. The faces wore sentimental expressions typical of Victorian art. I never tired of gazing at this piece.

Miss Liza was a neat erect women of slight frame with greying hair. She was always patient with children. She would never hurry my choice when I went into her store to buy a birthday or a Mother's Day present.

Miss Liza had an air of respectability and seemed to me a keeper of civilization.

CHAPTER TEN

My mother collected antiques in a small way. She would buy a piece of furniture or an old lamp from time to time; however, we spent a lot of time in antique shops and at auctions. This was fine with me in that such places would often have an old musket or a Civil War sword.

One day we were in Easton doing the weekly grocery shopping when I sighted an auction set up on the lawn of Mr. Edwards' place. He was a funeral director and auctioneer carrying out his business from a massive old clapboard L-shaped house across from the Episcopal Church.

It was a dry, clear June day. The furnishings of some great house were spread out on the picket-fenced lawn under huge old oak trees.

Large ancient family portraits were leaning against pieces of furniture or trunks of the trees. There were piles of brass andirons and tools, groups of elaborately carved dining chairs, worn old wing chairs, Empire card tables, a massive dining table, and countless small tables and chests of drawers.

The auction began before I could find Mr. Edwards and ask him if there were any old guns in the sale. In a thorough search I had found none. Mother promised we would return to Mr. Edwards on a day he wasn't so busy.

The smells and sights of that sale haunted me. I had never

before seen such a profusion of wonderful objects. One of the portraits was of a lady in a long gown with her hair done up in a wonderful antique manner.

The auction sent my imagination going with daydreams of plantation life, sailing ships, the Revolutionary War, all the things I knew and suspected about life two hundred years before.

ೞ

A couple of weeks later we called on Mr. Edwards. He sold a few antiques out of a couple of sparsely furnished rooms. An old, slant-front desk flanked by ladderback arm-chairs stood against one wall. There were no curtains at the six, over six windows. Even so, the rooms were dim because of the many old trees shading the house. An oval gate-leg table with a small oriental rug spread on its top stood at the center of the larger room.

Mr. Edwards picked up a brass-stocked, Miquelet-lock, "rat-tail" handled Turkish pistol. The price was twenty-five dollars, way outside my range. I asked if he had anything else.

He went to the corner and brought back a Springfield 1842 musket, the standard long-arm of the Mexican War. The price was five dollars. I looked it over from its mellow, old walnut stock to the great arc of its trigger guard, to its long barrel with steel bands. It was to be mine.

As we drove back to Oxford my mother explained that this gun would be my main birthday present. I couldn't be happier.

My pleasure in this old musket came, I think, from the easy associations I gave it with America's past. I had loved old things since early childhood. I could sit for hours and listen to my grandfather and his friend "Uncle George" talk about the Civil War, their parents' war, and the War of 1812, their grandparents' war. War was History in America in 1948.

CHAPTER ELEVEN

A ferry runs between Oxford and Bellevue on the opposite shore of the Tredavon. Mother and I were making our way from Saint Michaels back to Oxford. She decided to take the ferry in order to avoid the long drive via Easton and to give me the treat of the ferry ride.

The road wound to Bellevue through sweet countryside, passing through the village of Royal Oak with its white clapboard Methodist Church and one-room schoolhouse.

As we neared the ferry dock we spied a sign reading "Antiques" and an arrow pointing down a long driveway that followed the river. We turned in through terra-cotta-belted globe-form gateposts. The driveway ended in a circle, the main house straight ahead, and the antique shop, a small cabin to the right. Another sign read, "Ring bell".

A few minutes later a small, smiling woman came down from the direction of the main house. We were shown into the little white-washed cabin, and in a corner stood a Springfield 1864 rifled musket and cartridge box with strap and round brass eagle plate. The price was five dollars; the cartridge box was a dollar more. I had that much in my piggy bank and a deal was struck.

Mrs. Valliant, the owner of the shop, said to me, "I have a son who must be about your age. Would you like to meet him?"

I walked, on her instructions, around the driveway toward the main house, a tall, Victorian, shingled house painted white with green trim. A long screened porch ran along the back, in front of which stood Joe. He was slightly smaller than I, with light brown hair. There was an expression of good natured mischief on his face. I liked him right away.

CHAPTER TWELVE

It was agreed that two days hence I would take the ferry over from Oxford and spend the day at Joe's.

The day came and I mounted my bike and headed for the ferry dock at the far end of Oxford. I could see the ferry sitting at its dock on the opposite shore.

To alert the Captain one raised a sign which ran up a timber ladder-like structure when a rope was pulled. I did this and tied off the rope. After a couple of minutes I could see the ferry pull away from its berth. It took about ten minutes to cross the Tredavon. It pulled into the dock with the engines reversing and its sides glancing off tall posts which formed a water alley leading to the ramp, which was raised and lowered by chain pulleys.

Three cars lumbered off the ferry, up the ramp and off the dock on to the street below the Robert Morris Inn. I rolled my bike onto the ferry and paid my 25¢ round trip fare. I leaned against the rail and watched the river as we pulled out of Oxford. We had taken on a farm truck and three other passengers on foot.

Once we had docked, I helped move the guard chain to the side so the farm truck and the rest of us could get on our way. I pedaled down the long dock and on to the blacktop road.

CঙЗ

Next to a clapboard house at the first turn in the road was a post, on which stood a large old cannon-ball. It seemed that everywhere I turned there were artifacts that fired my imagination. I liked the house with its lace-curtained windows and the old shade trees which surrounded it, but the cannon-ball was the thing. Had this place been bombarded during the War of 1812? It would be one of the things I asked Joe about.

I rode down the Valliants' driveway and up to the main house. I knocked at the front door and was beckoned by his mother to another door further along the house. This door led to a room off the kitchen with a small table at which Joe was finishing his breakfast. He sprang up and said, "Let's go outside. I'll show you around the place."

Joe led me out another door next to which stood several shotguns. I was in a side yard. The Tredavon river was to my left, in front of the house; and ahead of me, across a small field, was a shallow creek bounded by tall reeds.

We turned around and walked behind the house, and passed an ancient building of large irregular clapboards and a peaked shake-shingled roof about twelve feet square, which looked much older than the main house. I found out, years later, that this old outbuilding was contemporary with the old main house, which had been destroyed by fire in the nineteenth century and rebuilt on the old foundations in the Victorian style.

Further on was a modern wooden garage and next came the antique shop I remembered from my last visit.

We walked down the oyster shell-paved drive until we

came to the barn. Joe walked me around to the cow stalls. He stroked the back of one of the cows and I did the same with some trepidation. This was my first time near cows and I was afraid of them. The cows were intent on their feed so they remained still.

We climbed to the hayloft and sat in the doorway with our legs hanging down, watching the cows go out of the barn below our feet. We could see most of the farm from this vantage point. Flat fields spread out in front of us. To the right was the tiny village of Bellevue. Joe's uncle had the general store and post office which was the largest building on the road which skirted the village.

We left the barn and continued down the drive heading for the general store. As we turned on to the road and left Joe's driveway we could just see the cannon-ball on the post.

"What is the story behind that cannon-ball?"

"Somebody just found it and stuck it on that post."

"I, thought, maybe, the British had bombarded Bellevue in the War of 1812."

"No, they bombarded Saint Michael's, or almost bombarded Saint Michael's." Joe went on to explain that a man named Jacob Gibson spotted the British fleet anchoring off the town at night. He hung lanterns in an apple orchard. The British were fooled by the ruse and fired on the orchard, with only a couple of rounds hitting the town.

☙

We ambled on to Joe's uncle's store. We climbed the dusty unpainted steps through the double screen doors, which had painted tin plates on them advertising "Blue Ribbon Bread" and "Seven-Up".

The interior was dim. There were several men sitting in firehouse chairs toward the back of the store. Floor-to-ceiling shelves ran along the left wall, with a long counter in front.

Joe said, "Uncle, this is my new friend Johnny."

"Hi there, young fellow," said Joe's uncle.

"Hello, Sir."

His face seemed to light up at my addressing him as "Sir", and at the same instant I knew that I had identified myself as a city boy.

Joe lifted the lid of a freezer and asked me what kind of ice cream on a stick I wanted. He pulled out two, holding them high for his uncle to see.

"You boys go ahead and take those ice creams and enjoy them."

We spent the afternoon wandering around the Valliant farm, talking as we went. We returned to Joe's house for supper. Mrs Valliant had killed a Guinea hen and had fried it. There were mashed potatoes and fresh peas from her garden. This was the best fried chicken I had ever tasted. I cleaned my pieces down to the bone and then sucked on the bones.

అ

Several days later I was talking to Mother about what I had learned from Joe about Jacob Gibson hanging lanterns in an orchard outside of St. Michaels to fool the British.

"Jacob Gibson was my great great uncle and your great

great great uncle. He was always anti-British because, I hear, of his experiences during the War of 1812. He owned two farms on the Easton Road; you've seen the gateposts with their names, 'Jena' and 'Austerlitz', two of Napoleon's great victories. However, across the Easton road from Uncle Jacob lived an Anglophile who named his farm 'Waterloo'."

CHAPTER THIRTEEN

The week following Joe came over to spend the night. Mother and I met the ferry at the appointed time. I had been looking forward to Joe's visit for days.

The sky was full of low dark grey clouds and the water was rippled in a way that Mr. Hobbs said forecasted storms. I said to Joe, "I hope the weather doesn't ruin our fun today."

"I can think of some things we can do if it rains."

As we drove toward Jack's Point the wind picked up, and as we got out of the car the first big drops of rain began to fall.

While running for the house my mother shouted, "Boys, help me close all the windows in the main house and the cabin."

We dashed around pulling windows down. The rain now was pouring. Driven by a wind from the river, the rain ran in rivulets down the now closed windows.

Joe asked my mother for some brown paper bags, pencils, and a pair of scissors.

"Johnny, let's draw pictures of war ships on these paper bags and then cut them out."

He went on to say that we could have a naval battle using the living room rug as the ocean.

We got to work drawing and cutting out our fleets. We each had a brown grocery bag to work with. We were setting up our ships just as the sun reappeared. The storm had moved on. We left our paper ships for another time and headed outside.

Water was running off of everything. The bushes around the house dripped loudly and the trunks of the trees were dark with rain. Soon the sun began to dry the rain away. A mist rose from the grass. The smell produced by earth and plants filled our nostrils.

☙

Mother called us in for dinner. Summer meals were often cold: sliced tomatoes, potato salad, and slices of baked ham.

After dinner we drove into Easton to see a movie. There were two theaters: the Easton and the Avalon. The Avalon was the grander of the two. This night we went to the Easton Theater. I noticed that the balcony was reserved for "Colored".

We watched a Randolph Scott western with double cartoons, newsreel, and lots of previews. In those days there were no movies on Sunday, so Saturday night was the last show of the week, and leftover previews or shorts were shown. I was hungry for every foot of film they could give me.

CHAPTER FOURTEEN

In Colonial times the harbor at Oxford was behind the present town. Of the old houses in Oxford only one remains. The rest of the seventeenth and eighteenth century buildings are gone.

It is hard to tell that once Oxford was not only the principal town of the Eastern Shore, but one of two ports in the state. By 1760 the port of Oxford went into decline. The great trees that line Oxford's main street give a hint at the town's former importance.

In the time I came to know Oxford it was a sailboat-building center with four or five boatyards. There were a couple of seafood processing plants where the watermen of the town sold their catches. Mother often bought crabs at the plants at bargain prices.

Sometimes I would ride my bike along the waterfront of the town to see what was going on. Several times I managed to be at the docks when watermen were coming and unloading, and weighing their catches. There was shouting and the scraping of the wheels of the pushcarts. The prices of various categories of crabs were written on a chalkboard at the end of the dock. The price changed a few pennies per bushel daily.

I recognized Mr. Hobbs as his boat pulled into the dock. He gave me a friendly wave as he tied up. He was very business-like. He handed up his bushel baskets to the waiting hands on the dock. I counted 19.

Mr. Hobbs climbed up the ladder to the dock and watched the grading of his catch. He signed something and was handed cash. He tucked the money in his shirt pocket and climbed back down the ladder and headed across the creek for home.

I watched Mr. Hobbs' boat pull away. I then cast my eye around the dock for a place I could sit and watch the goings-on. I put my back to one of the pilings a few feet from the front of the pier, a perfect vantage point.

The work boats were lined up three or four in a row, and the watermen were shouting back and forth to one another.

"Hal meny boushels you get today Elmer?"

"Morn I can count." came the reply.

"Hal they runnin?"

"Pleny ub em but they choosey, all thay wont is fresh ele."

"Couldn't fine no sof crayb today, teys all pealers and paper shells."

CHAPTER FIFTEEN

Near Trappe was an old ruined brick church.
A tall corner with parts of two walls was all that remained.
The place was called "Hole-in-the-Wall". It was, in fact, the
ruins of White Marsh Church, a Church of England parish
built in the seventeenth century.

Old gravestones stood in the overgrown yard, and very
near the ruined walls were two raised graves with large
rectangular horizontal stones. One was inscribed "Robert
Morris". He was heir to a large English trading company and
had lent his considerable fortune to support the American
Revolution.

CHAPTER SIXTEEN

I rode my bike to Joe's with a change of clothing and toothbrush in an old canvas knapsack I had found at Jack's Point. Again I crossed the Tredavon by means of the ferry.

I never tired of these ferry rides. The river was ever changing. The swells might be a little larger, the color would be a little greener, or depending on the sky, change its color altogether. New creatures could be seen swimming near the surface. When we pulled into the dock on the other side of the river it was always like being awakened from a dream.

It was a cloudy morning and it looked like it was about to rain. Since we would be inside that day, Joe asked his father if he could show me the gun collection in the upstairs study. We mounted the steep staircase and turned right into the study.

It took my breath away. Along several walls were rows of antique fowling pieces. Hanging in racks on the walls were Pennsylvania long rifles, both percussion and flintlock.

To my left was an old double-glazed-door bookcase filled with better antique long-arms and a shelf crowded with pistols of all kinds. As Joe closed the door behind he pointed to a pair of Mexican War Holster pistols in their original leather and brass saddle holsters, hanging from a coat hook.

A corner cupboard across the room was filled with minia-ture carvings of waterfowl done by Mr. Valliant. Interspersed with the carved birds were some of his finer antique pistols.

On the wall to my right was a large Victorian three-part bookcase with glazed doors. Inside it on shelves were hundreds of stone Indian arrowheads, axe heads, and other Indian relics.

I walked over to the corner cupboard. It was an antique made of pine with two thirteen-pane glazed doors. I pressed close to see what was inside. There on the bottom shelf rested a pair of Derringer pistols, the same sort John Wilkes Booth had used to assassinate President Lincoln. In spite of their sad history they were beautiful little things. The small stocks were finely carved and inlaid with silver.

Sitting around these Derringers on the shelf were small wood carvings of the waterfowl of the kind to be found on the Tredavon. These carvings were painted to simulate plumage. These were done to a professional standard and at the time I took for granted Mr. Valliant's skill.

ﬁ§

We pored over the weapons and artifacts in this room until the sun shone through the window. The clouds were breaking up; we were going to have a fine day after all. We went outside and got on our bikes.

Flat fields spread on either side of the road, obscured once in a while by privet or stands of pine trees planted as windbreaks. Along the left side of the road tall grasses grew, and sticking out of these grasses was a stone inscribed "V 1934". Joe said that this stone was a boundary marker put down by his father when the adjoining Willis farm was bought.

We rode past the one-room school in Royal Oak where Joe had gone for the first couple of grades. It was by this school the road split. To the left lay St. Michaels and to the right lay the Easton road and our destination. We passed small houses near the road and gateposts of farms and manors which lay across the fields, out of sight by the water.

Nature was fragrant that morning. The smells came roaring into my nostrils: wheat, corn, honeysuckle, wild rose, barley, rye, soybean, and boxwood. The air was full of scent and light.

We came to a long straight piece of road which was flanked by tall trees, making the road look like a tunnel. The road was a narrow two lanes, and the branches of the tall trees on either side of the road had grown together. The branches came down to a point where the tallest trunk's top would just touch. This stretch went on for about a mile, perspective making the road appear ever narrower toward the point of light at the end of the trees.

As we pedaled into this arboreal tunnel the light darkened and all became quiet. Shallow ditches on either side of the road were half filled with black water, and off beyond the rows of trees was a silent swampy forest. The atmosphere inspired my imagination and I began spinning a tale of ancient knights and villains. Joe spun a few tales of his own.

We came at last to the store. By this time I had worked up quite a thirst and went straight to the red cooler just inside the screen door. I came up with a long bottle of Nehi grape soda, a sweet purple concoction.

We pointed our bikes back toward Belleview. Not far from the store was our wooded tunnel, and again I was overcome by nostalgia and romance. As a little child my mother would take me for walks along the woodland paths which circulated through the unbuilt-upon parts of Roland Park, back in Baltimore. On these walks she would tell me stories sometimes or we would talk over the stories we had read. I suppose that is why the woods have a nostalgic effect on me. But this place was special.

I often have driven down this stretch of road to recapture that feeling from childhood. Maybe the car is moving too fast, or maybe it's because I'm in a car that I cannot recapture that romance. No, I think I can only be reminded of that feeling, I can't get back to my childhood again.

It's funny but the road looked different riding back. I recognized things but I was just as interested by the sights going back as I had been on the way out. Joe and I talked endlessly and time had wings.

CHAPTER SEVENTEEN

By the side of the ferry dock was a derelict factory. Some of its sides were leaning and part of the roof had collapsed. A rotting three-masted schooner sat in the shallow bottom next to the factory. This had been Joe's grandfather's establishment.

We leaned our bikes against a fence and walked around to the entrance to the factory. A heavy chain and padlock barred the front door, so we climbed through an open window. Joe said, "We're not supposed to be in here, so be careful."

The place smelled musty; the wooden floor was slightly canted and I could hear the water lapping against the pilings on which the building partly rested.

We were standing in a large room half the size of a football field. A row of mullioned windows looked out on the ferry dock. Bolted to the floor were rows of zinc tables and behind them were old zinc tubs and spigots. Joe explained that this had been the work room where crabs were picked and oysters shelled.

We explored the river side of the building with its derelict cold storage lockers and docks. At the other end of the building were the offices behind glazed panels.

The offices stood looking like we had entered them during a weekend break. The wire baskets stood full of papers. The desks were neat with fresh blotter paper. I opened one of the desks and found the drawer loaded with rubber stamps, reading: "Paid in full", "Please receipt and return", and "Property of William H. Valliant & Brothers". In the same drawer was an old pocket notebook/wallet with a printed calendar and railroad schedule for the years 1866 through 1876.

I asked Joe, "Is any of this stuff up for grabs?"

"Sure, take what you want. Nobody else wants it."

I put the old pocket book and several hand stamps in my pockets. I gave the old adding machine handle a crank or two before we climbed out the window.

Across the courtyard stood another large building with a conveyer belt angling up to a loft. "That place is where they made fertilizer out of oyster shells."

At dinner that night Joe mentioned to his father that we had been in the old factory. He cautioned us not to go there again because the place could fall in at any time and it would worry him to think of us in there.

☳

When I got home I took out my old pocket book. It had that wonderful smell of old things. The aged morocco leather of which it was made had a feel that new leather could not approach.

This object was a touchstone for me. I could imagine myself on a passenger train in 1870 speeding from Baltimore to New York, or paying for a dinner in a glittering gas-lit restaurant by producing huge old-style banknotes. I put several receipts in the wallet on which I had stamped "Paid" with one of the old hand stamps I had taken out of the factory.

CHAPTER EIGHTEEN

About once every summer we went to visit Mother's Aunt Sally Gibson who lived in Easton. Aunt Sally occupied a bedroom and bath on the first floor.

A bony woman with dark brown hair streaked with grey, she wore old fashioned round glasses. Her double bed was cluttered with pillows and notebooks. The tops of the bedside tables were covered with framed faded photographs of peoples' heads.

Aunt Sally was pleasant and not a bore. She never discussed her ailments; she seldom discussed herself at all, but asked questions about our lives.

Often I would leave Aunt Sally and Mother together. I would try to find Ralph, her grandson.

Ralph had a Japanese rifle his father had brought back from the war in the Pacific. It was a 6.5 mm carbine complete in every detail. There was a dust cover on the bolt action, a half-round piece of metal covering the action, and its old brown leather sling.

The sixteen-leaf chrysanthemum mark, which the Japanese used on their firearms, was intact. Quite often these had been filed down by American armorers to obliterate signs of Imperial Japan when the arms were surrendered or gathered after a battle. But when an individual soldier took a weapon no such filing off took place.

I didn't covet this carbine, but I was glad I could look at it when we visited Aunt Sally. I was learning by handling old weapons. I discovered that I learned best by being able to put my hands on a thing. I could get something from a book, but if I'd seen and touched a thing it became part of me. I didn't have to think about it. The knowledge was there for me. It was like the difference between reading a map and walking over the country it described.

The Wallbridge house was a two-and-a-half story brown shingle. It stood on a small piece of ground with grass and a couple of cedar trees. The house was on the south side of town near the fashionable section of Easton.

Ω

Once when the Wallbridges were to be away and Mother was going to visit Aunt Sally, I brought my bike along. I said my hellos to Aunt Sally before going outside and climbing aboard my Raleigh three-speed to explore Easton.

I headed toward the heart of town where stood the old red brick courthouse. An iron fence surrounded the building and bordered its brick sidewalks. Near the front door was a cast bronze tablet with a list of Talbot County's Confederate dead.

Mother said that when she was a child, public hangings were taking place outside this courthouse, and on a visit to Easton she had glimpsed such a hanging through the crowd which had gathered to watch. I tried to imagine what a hanging would be like. What would it be like to witness such a death? I was envious of my mother's sighting the event.

From the courthouse I turned left past the Easton Movie Theater. The marquee read, "Flying Leathernecks. Starts Weds.".

I rode on toward the Friends Meeting House, very near the road to Oxford. At the end of a residential street stood a row of tall bushes, a driveway and a sign reading "Third Haven Meeting".

I went through an opening in the hedge and followed the driveway as it curved toward a story-and-a-half shake-shingled peaked-roofed clapboard building, painted white. Four windows and two doors were cut into the side of the building facing me. A windowed porch protruded from the end of the building near the drive.

A silver and black iron historical marker stated that the parish had begun in 1676 and that the building had been completed in 1684. I stood there in this shaded grove looking at the Quaker Meeting House for some time.

I felt here a relief from the world. The atmosphere was very different from what I felt elsewhere on the Eastern Shore. This Third Haven Meeting House seemed a holy place to me. I had no words to describe "holy". I felt that in this place my higher self could be released.

I pedaled back to Aunt Sally's. As we drove home to Oxford I told mother about my ride and what I had seen. I wasn't able to tell how I felt about the Friends Meeting House. I just said that I liked the place and that I thought it was beautiful. She replied that she would like to go there sometime with me.

Many years later I came to know a few Friends and through them came to understand that when a person spoke up at a Meeting the speaker was a conduit for the words of a spirit. Knowing that the Friends had a belief in an inner light made me hunger for such a faith.

Not long ago I was given a small book printed to celebrate the two hundred and fiftieth anniversary of the Third Haven Meeting House in 1932. In that book was a list of surnames mentioned in records of from 1676 to 1894. Pearson was on the list as well as many other family names of ancestors. At the end of this booklet was this small poem:

> *"And so, I find well to come*
> *For deeper rest in this still room*
> *For here the habit of the soul*
> *Feels less the outer world's control;*
> *The strength of mutual purpose pleads*
> *More earnestly our common needs;*
> *And from the silence multiplied*
> *By these still forms on either side,*
> *The World that time and sense have known,*
> *Falls off and leaves us God alone."*

CHAPTER NINETEEN

My Uncle George and Aunt Jean came to visit for the weekend. They were an ancient couple, cousins of my grandparents.

Uncle George, sitting on a lawn chair looking out toward the creek with me sitting at his feet, told a story of his early days selling harness and such gear, traveling from town to town in Kentucky and Tennessee. He would set out from Baltimore by train and hire a horse and wagon, and in the period of a week visit twenty or thirty general stores in towns in the region of Nashville. He told of the winding dirt roads and the hill people with their corn-cob pipes and black hats.

Uncle George had a great deep voice and made discreet gestures as he talked. His eyes shone as he remembered details. He had the talent for bringing everyone listening into the story.

Uncle George was a lover of the human race. His remembrances were filled with details about what the people were like. The characters in his stories always had their reasons for doing what they did. Everybody was important in the scheme of things. He knew the names of all of the policemen on the beat around his factory. He knew all the firemen down at the firehouse. He remembered everybody's birthday, if not with a gift, certainly with a word of congratulation. He and Aunt Jean were happy people.

CHAPTER TWENTY

While riding into Easton for weekly grocery shopping, I would turn on the car radio and there find only the twanging sounds of country music, but songs by Hank Williams were wonderful. Occasionally "bluegrass" tunes by Bill Monroe or Mac Wiseman would be played. These I loved too. The sound of country music of the 50's crept into my memory, and when I hear such songs today it sometimes takes me back to those days outside Oxford.

The ESSO station on the way to Easton was operated by a couple who also operated a small general store selling bread, milk, etc. On the counter was a punch board. You paid a nickel and punched a peg in one of the many holes on the board with the hope you would land on a prize hole. This punch board tempted me in no way and I was always curious why adults would waste nickels punching holes. I never saw a winner nor did I ever hear of one. I used to ask, "Has anybody won on that punch board?" The answer was always, "Not so far."

Outside by the gas pumps the owner kept a portable radio tuned in to country music. One day while we were getting the car gassed up, this radio of his was blasting Hank's "Hey, hey, good-lookin. What's ya got cookin? How's about cookin somthin up with me? . . . " I could picture someone driving up and leaning out the window of a hot rod talking to a gal just this way.

CHAPTER TWENTY-ONE

One day while I was visiting Joe we pedaled our bikes to his Aunt Frida's. The place was on a point off the road to Royal Oak.

We passed on our way a sign for "Clay's Hope 1692". A tall hedge grew all along the road front of this place so that nothing could be seen of the house.

My curiosity got me to call to Joe to stop. I was going to look through the hedge to see what was behind it. I wanted to see what a house from 1692 looked like. I pushed leaves and branches out of the way and stuck my head into the hedge, At the bottom of a lawn stood a white clapboard house of no particular distinction or interest.

"Joe, there is nothing special about that house. I thought one that old would look different or better, somehow."

"On our way back from Aunt Frida's I'll take you to my Uncle Al's place. He lives in a real interesting old house."

Joe's Aunt Frida lived in a big old clapboard three-story house called "Grand Haven" which stood on a wide point of land in the Tredavon river, looking south and east. There were only a couple of old trees on the property; therefore light was everywhere.

The house was clean and neat to the point that it didn't look like an Eastern Shore house, but I liked the look of the place.

We went inside through the kitchen door. Joe's Aunt Frida was wiping her hands on a linen towel. When dry she put her right hand forward and shook mine while saying welcome.

"Boys, lunch will be in about twenty minutes; so why don't you take a look at our new boat? I'll call you when everything is ready."

We strolled down the long yard toward the pier. Tied up there was a new 20-foot motorboat. White-painted hull, mahogany railings, hatches, and brass hardware all glistened in the sun.

Neither of us said much about the boat. It looked pretty. What more was there to say?

Frida stuck her head out of the door and called us to lunch. We ate in the large dining room with bright sunlight streaming through the windows. I was asked lots of questions about school and life in Baltimore.

I discovered over lunch that Frida's husband, who was in Easton that day, had been the president of the Reading Railroad. I thought of the many Monopoly games I had played, and a Chance card that read "Take a ride on the Reading". I liked the idea that the Reading really existed and was run by a flesh and blood person.

☾

After lunch at the hands of Aunt Frida we were off to Uncle Al's place. Where the road turned left toward Belleview we continued on straight.

A wind was blowing about 15 knots from the south, right

in our faces. It was hard pedaling after a big lunch and a huge slice of chocolate cake. The sky was darkening and it had cooled down.

The oyster shell road turned right at the water. The tide was at its highest and the yard around the house looked no more than a foot above the creek's waters. The darkening sky made the white of the house's clapboards bright and chalky.

The house telescoped down in three sections. The oldest part was a vertical two-and-a-half stories, with a steep shake roof with a huge chimney. The middle section was two stories as well, but smaller with a gentle slant to its roof. The last part was one story and enclosed the kitchen. Again a large chimney was attached to the end of that building.

Joe's uncle came to the kitchen door and asked us in. As he and Joe talked I took the place in. We walked through the dining room into the living room. A large staircase went up the wall between the dining and living rooms and turned at a right angle to reach the second floor.

At the end of the living room stood the largest fireplace I had ever seen. A heavy curved molding surrounded the fireplace opening without a mantel shelf. The walls were paneled and painted a dark color. The window sills were deep and the windows small for the size of the room.

This living room was the whole first floor of this section of the house. The front windows looked out at the water, and the tide being so high all I could see was water. It was like being on a ship. In the opposite wall were two windows looking out on fields.

A gentle rain began to fall which gave the green of the grass a luminous sheen.

The look and feel of this house seemed to me to be the essence of the Eastern Shore. The play between the land and the water gave this house a perfection I had never seen before. There had been many places that had caught my eye and interest, but this house stirred something deeper. It was as if there was an ancient memory of this place in my body, not in my head.

CHAPTER TWENTY-TWO

The Oxford Yacht Club ran sailing lessons. We didn't belong to the club but non-members could take instruction for a fee. Mother signed me up. All the students were around the same age. I was eleven at the time.

The club owned a number of small boats called Oxford Sailors, an open boat about 14 feet in length with a center board and single mast. They were made of plywood stretched over a hardwood frame and were quite light by the standards of the day. I could turn the boat over to clean the bottom and could put it in the water by myself. That is what we did every morning of the two-week course. Once in the water we would drop the center board which was a small drop-down keel, and raise the sail.

The instructor was impeccably turned out each day. White military-looking shorts, an ironed white shirt, long white socks, white boating shoes, and topping the whole thing off with a white cotton hat with the brim turned down all the way around. The light would catch his greying English military-style mustache. He stood at the end of the club's L-shaped dock and shouted instructions through a megaphone.

He would get us sailing in a tight circle and then shout through his megaphone, "Stat yo-ar tack". This meant that we were to tack out of the circle and take independent courses, and then return to the circle on the opposite tack, or turn.

He taught us well. He played no favorites and abided no horseplay. A gifted teacher who knew his subject well. I still remember the nomenclature of boat parts, lines, and sails he drilled into our heads. He taught us how to read the wind's direction and how to hold a sail and the tiller to best use that wind.

After a time it became my second nature to sail, much like riding a bike. However, the experience was more like flying. The quiet of a sailboat moving through the water propelled only by wind is one of the world's great pleasures.

On Sundays my teacher and his wife, who looked to be cut from the same piece of cloth, would be out on their 25-foot sailboat *Circe*. Both in their sun-faded often-washed clothes, their faces relaxed. They had that English Colonial look. They would spend their whole day sailing or stay out as long as the wind lasted. Good wind was not a constant feature of Eastern Shore summers.

CHAPTER TWENTY-THREE

Often my mother and I would go off for a day of exploration, to see places like the Wye Oak, or the town of Crisfield. Once or twice we spent a day in Ocean City, walking the boardwalk and swimming in the ocean, and polishing the whole thing off with a cup of French-fried potatoes bought from a boardwalk vendor and eaten while hot looking out at the sea.

One morning we set off for Old Trinity Church on Church Creek outside of Cambridge. The route took us out the Easton road and then by the town of Trappe, which brought us out onto the Easton-Cambridge leg of Route 50. All these roads were very flat, and we passed endless fields of corn and soybeans. The tires made a "thump thump" sound as we rolled down the concrete highway.

A mile or two before the road gets to the bridge over the Choptank River, a pine forest comes into view. These cool, fragrant pines always came as a tremendous relief after the heat of the rest of that stretch of highway.

The bridge over the Choptank brought us to the edge of Cambridge. At the center was a drawbridge section with guardhouses. There was a lot of river traffic and the draw-bridge was often up. Long waits would ensue. Everyone would shut their engines off and get out of their cars to stretch and discuss with each other how long the bridge would be up.

Along both sides of the bridge stood fishermen with their tackle boxes and buckets on the sidewalks, many with several poles wedged into the railings and their lines trailing in the water below. Many of the black fishermen were using simple bamboo poles but seemed to be catching as many, if not more, fish than their better-equipped white counterparts.

ଓଃ

Eventually the bridge would lower, and we would start moving again. We turned right for Church Creek.

The town of Church Creek was truly old, many houses having gambrel roofs and dormer windows. All were in poor and rundown condition. "What a treasure trove," I thought. I could picture men at work repairing rotting boards and applying fresh coats of paint, ending up with something to rival Williamsburg.

We turned back to Trinity Church. Surrounded by the waters of Church Creek on three sides, it is separated from the road by an old iron fence. The church is brick and has a high-pitched shingle roof. The building is T-shaped with no bell tower. The doors and windows were Gothic arched, which gave the place a look far older than its building date of 1680.

The churchyard was perfect. It looked the way I had always pictured a churchyard. The grass sloped to the still waters of the creek, and rows of old, moss-grown gravestones stood among the ancient trees.

I found the grave of Thomas King Carroll, a former

governor of Maryland, and his daughter. Her stone read, "Anna Ella Carroll, Born August 29, 1815. Died Feb. 19th 1893. 'The Greatest Woman of her Time.' " I looked around at the other stones but was haunted by the inscription "The Greatest Woman of her Time". I had never heard of her and was eager to learn more about her.

We went into the church and took in its quiet, damp, white-washed interior. On the wall over the door was painted, in large block letters, a list of those one was not to marry: "Not your sister, not your cousin, not your aunt, not your brother, not your father", etc.

 beginsmidt ❧

We stopped on the road for a supper at a roadside stand just before the Cambridge side of the Choptank river. The counter man spoke in a deep accent of the region, "Royt, what kine of burger do yah wont."

Mother replied, "Two with fried onions."

"Royt, two with froyed onyons."

We drove back to Oxford when the sun was low in the sky.

I made a beeline for the encyclopedia. No Anna Ella Carroll. I pulled a couple of American histories off the shelf and again could not come up with anything on the lady.

Next time in Easton I would inquire at the library. There I found a book titled *My Dear Lady* by Marjorie B. Grenbie, published in 1940. This book told at great length who Anna Ella Carroll was. She had been a political writer in the 1840-60 era and a backer of Lincoln, and after Lincoln's election, an advisor to the President and to his military commanders. All very unusual for a woman in the mid-nineteenth century.

I think that Maryland being, in many ways, a southern state, and unwilling to make too much of any effort on behalf of the Union cause; combined with the fact that the U.S. Congress would not recognize her status with a pension or payment for her services to the country, the light of Anna Ella Carroll's reputation had been kept under a bushel. Even today she is virtually unknown.

I as a child was very sympathetic to the Confederate cause. None the less, I was very intrigued by Anna Carroll, especially by the fact that she had planned the Union forces' strategy in the West along the Tennessee, as well as many other large military campaigns. Lincoln admitted that he could not let it be known that "the armies of the United States were moving under the direction of a civilian" (a woman).

CB

One day Mother arranged that a girl, whom I had never heard of nor had seen, spend the day with us on a day trip to Tunis Mills. She had met this girl on one of her visits to Aunt Sally and I think that she was a distant cousin.

We drove from Easton out the St. Michael's road and turned right toward Tunis Mills. I was looking forward to seeing Tunis Mills. The name carried a hint of Arab mystery. But Tunis Mills turned out to be just another jumble of plank and shingle houses. No Mill, no Tunis.

CHAPTER TWENTY-FOUR

Joe came up from the Eastern Shore to visit us in Baltimore. We walked from my house up to the Roland Park Water Tower and rode the Number 10 electric bus down to the corner of Howard and Read Streets, by the Richmond Armory.

Across the street stood a row of antique shops. Harris's near the top of the block always had a small room lined with old rifles, muskets, and shotguns and several china cabinets crammed with antique pistols.

Mr. Harris was a sweet-tempered old man who liked children and let us pore over the guns for as long as we wanted. Mr. Harris had a strong Cockney accent which prompted Joe to ask Mr. Harris if he was from England. "Born in the East End of London, my boy. You've a keen ear."

We both had money for lunch and I suggested Chinatown. We picked the The New Canton Inn and ordered Chow Mein. This was a first for Joe but he dug into the food without hesitation. The meal was good and very cheap and it was a real pleasure to be on our own in a restaurant ordering, paying, and being treated like any other patron by the waiter. We sat gazing at the painted lanterns and other decorations, drinking tea and munching fortune cookies.

When we paid for lunch the day's newspaper was on the counter. We asked if we could look at the movie section. We decided on something showing at the Valencia, more to see the theater than the film. The Valencia was part of two theaters in the same building. The Century was on the street level and the Valencia was an elevator ride above.

The elevators were huge and would hold twenty-five people at once comfortably. The elevator operator called out coming attractions as the car slowly ascended. The doors parted as the operator said, "Watch your step. Seats to the left."

The Valencia was decorated in Spanish motifs of differing periods and tastes. Crossed spears held draperies over doorways. The walls were done in fake embossed leather and the plaster columns were gilded and painted. The floors were of a dark tile. Elaborately patterned carpet led down the grand staircase which we took on our way out.

We entered the theater. The place was huge. Bulging gilt boxes ran from the balcony to the edge of the stage. Gilt decoration was everywhere. A Moorish decor took over the walls and ceiling from which hung Mosque lamps, dimly glowing.

CB

The film feature finished in the middle of the afternoon and we ambled from the theater over to Charles Street and up to the Walters Art Gallery. The Walters, housed in a limestone copy of a Genoese palace, is a tall three-story square place on a steep hillside leading up to the tall cylindrical marble Washington Monument on what is called Mount Vernon Place.

Joe wanted to see Mount Vernon Place and I promised that

we would after we had taken in the wonders of the Walters. We entered through bronze and glass revolving doors into a marble lobby and then up marble steps to the main floor. We stood with our heads tilted back, looking at the skylighted ceiling fifty feet above. A colonnade supports a balcony on all sides of the room, and at the other end was another staircase leading up to the second floor.

All around the main room were Roman sculptures, a Roman well-head, and some heavily carved marble sarcophagi. Joe and I approached the well-head but found that it went no deeper than the floor. Off to both sides of this main room were smaller rooms containing collections of European and Etruscan art.

We strolled through the rooms and made our way to the stairs. Halfway up is a landing and on the wall there hangs a huge rectangular terra-cotta relief covered in enamel of many colors in the style of Luca Della Robbia. We paused to stare at the figures of Adam and Eve with the serpent in a tree which stood between them. Eve had the apple in her hand. I had loved this luminous piece from early childhood.

The upper floor of the Gallery was filled with paintings and bronzes. We strolled through these galleries and left the Walters. A few steps up the hill took us to Mount Vernon Place.

The street is paved in granite blocks and circles the grand column which is the Washington Monument. We entered the base and climbed the worn marble circular staircase which leads to the top of the monument. We looked out the small windows at the great view of the city in four directions.

Friday morning we set off for Oxford. There wasn't a huge line waiting for the ferry to cross the Chesapeake Bay and we quickly boarded the *Harry Nice*, one of four ferries named after Maryland governors.

Joe and I climbed over all the ferry's decks and explored its public cabins and looked under the covers of the lifeboats. When we docked, we saw Mother had fixed a picnic lunch. We drove to Joe's house and dropped him off and took the Tredavon ferry back to Oxford.

CHAPTER TWENTY-FIVE

Mother and I took the train for New York.
We each had a full suitcase to hand to the cab driver who took
us to Penn Station.

I wanted to use the Baltimore & Ohio railroad, but the B&O
had no right-of-way into New York City, its tracks terminating
in Hoboken, New Jersey. A B&O traveler then had to board a
ferry to cross the Hudson into New York.

Soon we were crossing the many rivers north of the city.
There were no side rails on the bridges. We seemed to be flying
over water. We sped north and arrived at Penn Station, New
York City.

We hauled our bags up and out to the cab stand. My
mother told the driver to take us to the Peter Cooper Hotel.
He didn't know the hotel and it took questioning several other
cab drivers. "Way Petera Coppera Otel?" Someone finally said
"Lex. and 39th Street."

This was my first time in a real big city hotel. It wasn't a
fancy place but it was fine by me. The bed had a high, hard
mattress and the bathroom was full of all kinds of towels. We
were on the tenth floor and I could see a long way up and
down Lexington Avenue.

There was a background hum to New York over which
short-term loud sounds would flare. There was the rumble of
subway trains coming up through the grates in the sidewalks,

the short horn blasts of taxis, the squealing of brakes, and an occasional shout.

We walked up Madison Avenue to 50th Street and went into "Hamburger Heaven" around two in the afternoon. On the walls there were silly looking cows in painted plaster here and there. The waitresses were brisk and to the point, but not rude or unfriendly, and fast beyond any quickness I had seen before.

My hamburger was big and juicy and tasted better than any I had had before. Mother said she thought they were made from a blend of round and sirloin. The french fries were from freshly cut potatoes and I followed these with a thick, ice cold, chocolate milkshake.

We walked the half block between the restaurant and Fifth Avenue and turned right and headed north past Saks, dodging the crowd and looking in the store windows.

The Rockefeller Center on the other side of Fifth Avenue was something quite wonderful. The ice skating pond was covered up with a board flooring waiting for its winter ice. Everything else about the place was as I had pictured it. A huge gilt statue hovers over the place.

We strolled back to our hotel. That evening we ate at a Hungarian restaurant on upper Second Avenue.

After a splendid meal of goulash we walked a long way down Second Avenue on our way back to the hotel. We stopped to peer in the windows of the shops and restaurants along the way. In a Viennese-style cafe we could see a man playing the zither and heard the strains of the "Third Man Theme".

Cʒ

The next morning we had a room-service breakfast. This was a first for me. A waiter brought everything on a rolling table with a white cloth trailing to the floor. Our plates had scrambled eggs and bacon, toast and rolls, coffee and cocoa, iced water, orange juice, and marmalade.

This was the morning we were going to visit Francis Bannerman and Sons at 501 Broadway. Bannerman's was a huge store selling antique and modern military surplus goods. It was founded in 1865 by buying government auction surplus and captured goods from the Civil War. Since that time Bannerman's had bought up goods from around the world and become a mecca for the collector.

A huge catalogue was put out every few years, and I had been poring through one for years, dreaming of the time I would visit the place. Inside the cover there was an announcement which read: "Attention Revolutionaries. We are able to outfit Revolutionary armies with everything from uniforms to gun boats."

There was page after page of photographs of muskets, rifles, cannons, gun boats, bombs, shells, carbines, swords, bayonets, medals, uniforms. Things were from the American Revolution, the Civil War, the Mexican War, the Indian Wars, the Spanish-American War, the English Colonial Wars, and the Franco-Prussian War. Up the Hudson river stood Bannerman's Island on which was stored the heavy ordinance.

The man at the hotel desk gave us directions to Bannerman's. We were to take the Lexington Avenue subway local to Spring Street, and when we emerged onto Broadway we should be only a block away. In fact we came up almost across the street from Bannerman's.

In those days Broadway and Spring Street was a run-down Victorian business and warehouse district. The store was housed in a five-story iron-front. Huge windows spread across the front of the building. Tall skinny double doors led in. I pressed the well-worn iron latch handle and pushed the giant door inward.

It took a couple of seconds for my eyes to get used to the dim interior. A man in a bow tie and suspenders asked us what we wanted. I said, "Old guns, uniforms, gun parts."

"You've come to the right place. There are three floors of showroom open. Lights are on. Make yourselves at home." The man offered Mother a chair which she took with pleasure.

I pulled a list out of my inner jacket pocket. On it were things I wanted that would fit into my twenty-five dollar limit. The only things that existed for me in those moments were the objects before me. The world had gone away. I was totally rapt in the profusion before me. Never before had I seen so many wonderful things.

There were endless racks of rifles, muskets, carbines. Shelves were lined with hundreds of cap and ball Civil War revolvers. Tables had stacks of Civil War jackets, hats, belts, canteens, cartridge boxes, bayonets and scabbards. Swords stood in barrels. Glass cases were filled with medals and decorations of all kinds.

I found a "Jeff Davis" cavalry hat, a cavalry jacket, a ram-rod for an 1842 Springfield musket. A bayonet for an 1862

Tower rifle. Two brass bullet molds, 36 and 44 caliber. It took me an hour and a half to find these objects while Mother patiently waited for me in her chair near the front door of the shop.

I put my finds on the counter. The total came to twenty-three dollars and fifty cents including New York sales tax. Everything was wrapped in brown paper and bound with string.

Mother and I carried the packages away and rode the subway back uptown to the Peter Cooper. We dropped my packages at the hotel and headed back to Hamburger Heaven for lunch.

ભ

The Metropolitan Museum was the afternoon's destination. We took a bus up Madison to 87th Street and walked west over to Fifth to the Museum. What a place. We walked up the grand stone stairway to the pillared main entrance and through revolving doors into the reception hall, where we bought tickets and were given a map of the exhibition halls.

We walked down a narrow hallway past the main staircase. The hallway was so humble compared with the rest of the place I wondered if we were lost. Along and set into the walls were lighted display cases filled with small objects from ancient Egypt.

At last we came out into a large dimly lit room filled with objects and portions of church interiors from the Gothic Period. Several stained glass windows were along the walls and were lit from behind.

We turned right and walked into a large room which housed the armor collection. There were at least twelve horse mannequins wearing armor, harness, and heraldic cloth decoration. Sitting in the saddles were human mannequins dressed in armor and carrying lances or swords. High on the walls hung heraldic banners of many colors. Beyond the horse displays were cases filled with every type of sword, battle axe, parts of armor, many helmets with chased decoration, and breast plates with gilt edges and scenic chasing.

We finally ascended the long staircase to the second floor to see the paintings. There was room after room filled with the best of America's collections of the paintings of the great masters through the works of the Impressionists. Then we found ourselves outside the main entrance looking down at Fifth Avenue.

Mother and I walked through Central Park from the museum down to 57th Street, to its southern boundary and then down Fifth Avenue to the Rockefeller Center again. We went into the Cafe and had supper.

The Rockefeller Center Cafe was simple and relaxed but everything was well done and the views out the plate glass windows to the skating pond and terraces were part of the New York of my daydreams.

CHAPTER TWENTY-SIX

It was the summer of 1954. We were on our way out of Baltimore by ten-thirty in the morning. Mother had gassed up and had the wagon serviced at Elburn's garage the day before.

Elburn ran a fine establishment. He and his men kept the cars of Roland Park rolling through the Depression and the Second World War and was doing a brisk business in the post-war boom. He knew how to treat people, and my mother, who was a bit frightened of cars, always felt secure in the hands of Elburn and assistants.

We moved through the city and across the Hanover Street Bridge to the Ritchie Highway which led to Annapolis and connected to the Chesapeake ferry road.

Between Annapolis and the ferry dock was a hamburger joint full of truck drivers munching burgers and playing the slot machines. I loved the place. They sold a great burger and milkshake, and I tried to get Mother to stop there every time we were on our way to the Eastern Shore. There was a low-ceilinged main room with a counter on three walls facing you, booths across the front, and tables in the center. Slot machines occupied the rest of the available space, but for a large claw machine next to the front door.

The claw machine had a wooden base; the upper part was glazed. Prizes like packs of cigarettes wrapped in dollar bills,

Zippo cigarette lighters, cast metal horses with cowboy saddles, decks of cards with colorful pinups on their backs filled the bottom. Looming over these was a gleaming chrome-plated mechanical crane with toothed jaws. Controls on the side of the base operated the crane, and for a nickel one was to pick up the desired prize and drop it down a chute which would deliver it out a slot to the winner. The place had great food.

We got to Easton around two in the afternoon and stopped at the A&P and stocked up on groceries for the empty refrigerator, which we called the "ice box", and the waiting shelves of the pantry.

Jack's Point didn't change from visit to visit. I helped mother unload the groceries and her suitcases. She helped me get the windows of my cabin open to let the musty smell out. She pulled the bedspread off and we both made the bed with fresh sheets brought down from Baltimore. She took the curtains down and threw them in a pile with the bedspread. These were washed and dried on the line.

CHAPTER TWENTY-SEVEN

My sister Ann and her nine-month-old daughter Van were coming for a visit. They arrived early in the afternoon. Van was in a car seat smiling and chattering baby talk. Ann brought a folding crib which we set up in the living room so Van could be put down for a nap after she was fed.

While Ann was getting settled in I took Van in my arms and walked with her around the grounds. I showed her the pier, my tree, my cabin, the back vegetable garden, and the flower beds which surrounded the house. She was a sweet child and didn't make a sound as I described what we were viewing. Her eyes got larger as I held her up to see this or that. It seemed to me that she was taking everything in.

That evening when Mother and Ann were unfolding the sofa-bed they found a mouse family living in the doubled-over mattress. The two of them were too soft-hearted to kill the creatures. Mother swept the whole little family into a shoebox and released them outside in the ivy patch.

CHAPTER TWENTY-EIGHT

The Valliant graveyard was an interesting old place with a rusted iron fence supported by brick columns. The 20-foot square was filled with gravestones. There were several tall obelisks but mostly the stones were the tall thin type. The Valliants' death dates spanned two hundred years with no recent arrivals.

We stopped by Joe's relatives' general store in Bellevue for a soda. We walked back to Joe's house kicking oyster shells and drinking our sodas.

I looked in the crowded window of Miss Liza's Shop and went into the Confectionary Store, a few doors further along, for a few penny candies, soft orange-colored marshmallow peanuts, big hard watermelon-shaped candies. From there we strolled past the old houses on the river side of town and then turned toward the Episcopal Church.

ॐ

A couple of days later, I found myself again across the river at Joe's. We sat under a tree in his front yard looking across at Oxford. He asked me what camp was like and I described the place and my tent mates. I thought he would be interested in my counselor's remembrances of World War II.

"We could get him to talk about the War sometimes during nap time in the afternoons after lunch, or at night after lights

70

out. He had been with the vanguard of Americans that liberated Belsen concentration camp."

Joe and I had seen pictures in *Life* magazine of what these places had looked like. My counselor said that they could smell Belsen before they could see it. Nothing in his life before had prepared him for what awaited him.

As the U.S. Army trucks came toward the camp some prisoners pressed against the barbed wire waving their arms and shouting. The gates were unlocked and the guard posts abandoned.

Penetrating the camp, they found mass graves and several large buildings full of corpses. The living prisoners were barely alive. One of the men handed out a bar of soap, which one of the prisoners quickly ate.

The camp guards were in several barracks buildings. They were brought outside where they were searched and put back inside under armed guard. Later that same day the guards were put to work burying the dead, which numbered in the thousands.

The magazine pictures and television programs about these places had not given me the reality of a first-hand story. Knowing someone who had seen these things made them very real for me.

My counselor had a pair of German army swimming trunks which he had gotten out of a warehouse found filled with Nazi uniforms and other supplies. He said that American forces were moving so quickly into Germany that all they were getting in supplies were ammunition and K rations. When he came upon an abandoned warehouse he found bundles of clean socks and underwear. He and his buddies filled their knapsacks and passed out these needed changes to other men in their battalion. The swimming trunks were part of that day's haul.

To my boyish mind war was about the experiences of the victors, not about the real gore, death, fear, and boredom. What I wanted was my chance to get some war loot.

CHAPTER TWENTY-NINE

Joe's father had often mentioned his trips to Smith Island, and he had whetted my curiosity about the place. I had pestered my mother about taking a trip down there.

Smith Island lies between Deal Island and Tangier Island in a part of the Chesapeake bay called Tangier Sound. A mail boat went from Crisfield every day in the summer but Sunday.

It would be a long trek. There would be a couple of hours driving to Crisfield, then the boat ride and the drive back home to Jack's Point.

It took us about an hour and a half to get to Salisbury, and these roads I knew well. But when we turned south from Salisbury I was in new territory. The road was lined with thick stands of tall pines mixed with maples, oaks, and poplars.

We pulled into Crisfield and asked a man in a gas station where we could catch the boat to Smith Island. He replied, "Royt at the end of the road; at town dock. You better hurr-eh, she leaves at eight thirt-eh."

We had about fifteen minutes. We found the town dock with no trouble. We saw the mail boat tied up at the pier right in front of where we parked the car. I shouted to the Captain, "Do you have room for two more?"

"I've plent-eh a room; take your toyme."

This way of talking was broader than that I heard in Oxford and the "hoy and oy" sound was much stronger.

The mail boat pulled away from the town dock and headed for Smith Island, straight across the sound. We passed numerous crab and oyster processing plants which lined the harbor.

The sky was tremendous and filled with cumulus clouds with a trailing white mist behind. In front of the clouds the sky was an intense blue. The sky was much bigger here.

Rain was forecast for that night but the bay was calm. It was my first time on the lower bay, and here it is much wider and closer to the ocean. The air and water were saltier than the waters further north.

CB

It took an hour to get to Ewell, one of three towns on the Island, with a good bit of that time spent passing the marsh-land which makes up three quarters of the mass of Smith Island. The noise of the boat's engines made conversation difficult. It was a relief to reach the dock, where the engines were cut.

Mother then asked the Captain if there was somewhere we could get lunch. "Ask in the town for Mrs. Evans' hoose. Everbody's named Evans so moyke it clar that you wont the Mrs. Evans that feeds tourists." He also added that for a couple of dollars we would be served a fine lunch.

It was now about ten o'clock and we had several hours before lunch and a good three-and-a-half hours before the boat went back to Crisfield. We ambled around the town for a while, and having found the house where lunches were served and looking at the place in general we decided to walk to

74

Rogue's Point. As we walked west out of the town we passed white picket fences and neat yards in front of the small peaked-roofed houses of the town. The place was quiet. Cats ambled around the occasional porch but birds were everywhere.

The road led through marshland. The place was flat and very low to the water. Sometimes when the bay could be seen it looked to be higher than the island. We crossed, on our way, two low wooden bridges with tidal water running quickly beneath our feet.

We came finally to Rogue's Point, in the middle of which was another Methodist Church with a graveyard full of old and new stones. Mostly Evanses, Dizes, and Tylers. In the back of the graveyard were some stones from the eighteenth century.

We walked around the town of Rogue's Point and looked at the soft crab dealers' piers. Here, as in Ewell and Crisfield, the soft crabs and pealers were held in zinc-lined wooden trays with sea water running in and out. Mother explained that soft crabs would only be in the soft shell state for a few hours, and the point of the trays full of water was to watch them while they shed their old shells. Once their shells were off they were taken to be packed in ice for their shipment to market.

We turned around and walked back to Ewell for lunch. We could see across the marshes another town to the south. Mother said it was called Tylerton.

☙

We arrived at the boarding house just as lunch was being served. There were two large tables with oilcloth covers, and four other people were already sitting down. Everybody said hello as we took our seats and got ready to eat crab cakes, stewed tomatoes, cornbread, fresh peas, and beans. Dessert would be a large slice of chocolate cake with iced tea to wash it down.

I asked a man I recognized as crew on the mail boat, "What do you call these flies with green heads and tan bodies?"

"We call em green heads. They only bite once in a wall. They stay for two weeks. We git a good starm and in comes a new bunch. They might be tan-ens or li'll black-ens. They breed out in the marshes. I guess the birds have to have somthin to eat."

We paid for lunch and strolled back to the boat. Again the sound of the engines isolated me into a world of my own. I looked at the sailing oyster boats, the skipjacks at anchor waiting for oyster season to begin in September. As we drew further out of Ewell I could see masts of skipjacks down in the harbor of Tylerton.

Several crab boats were returning from Crisfield where they had sold their catches. Out in the bay several motorboats bobbed at anchor with fishermen aboard.

CHAPTER THIRTY

In the late fall of that same year Joe asked me to come down to Cove Hall for some bird shooting. I packed up on a Friday and Mother drove me. She would be spending the weekend at Jack's Point and I would meet her on Sunday when the shooting was done.

I had new Bean boots and a warm field coat. I had gotten as a birthday present a pocket heater. It operated something like a Zippo cigarette lighter, but when you closed the lid it continued to smolder. It produced a fine warmth.

Saturday morning Joe and I were up with the sun. After breakfast we went up to the gun room where I picked out a double barreled twelve-gauge shotgun. Joe took a Winchester twelve-gauge pump.

Joe's father had gotten a German short-haired pointer we took with us to the fields along the Royal Oak Road, where there were supposed to be several coveys of quail.

It was bitter cold out and I shifted my pocket heater to a back pocket and pulled on my hat and gloves. The sky was a solid light grey, and all the vegetation was dead on the ground and had turned various shades of brown. The horizon was punctuated by the grey trunks and bare branches of sleeping trees.

The Valliants' pointer, without instruction, went to the far side of the field away from us and began to come forward, working back and forth, his nose to the ground. About fifteen yards from us he stopped, lifted a front paw and stuck his tail straight out.

"He's got a covey," Joe whispered. "Move quietly toward him. I'll shout to him and he will drive the birds out."

We crept foward a few paces. Joe shouted "Ho!"

With a loud beating of wings quail were everywhere. Joe fired once and brought down two birds. I had not gotten a shot off. I could not see where to shoot. The quail had flown out of cover in a twisting arc and it would take some watching to get the hang of their maneuvering. The trick of shooting quail, as I saw it, was to spot your bird and to anticipate its curving path and fire ahead of the bird.

We walked through two more fields. The cold was stinging my cheeks and ears and I had to rub my hands together. The cold was penetrating my gloves. I was wearing two pair of socks so my feet were still warm. I was glad of the water-proofing the rubber-soled lowers of my hunting boots gave.

The pointer was working toward us again when he stopped and pointed. Joe and I looked at each other and stepped quietly forward, guns at the ready. "Ho!" and up they flew.

I spotted my birds and was swinging left with my finger squeezing the trigger when Joe's head came into view. I lowered the gun with trembling hands. I had been a fraction of a second away from pulling the trigger and shooting Joe in the head. He was shooting at a quail away to his left and when he turned around he saw my pale face and asked, "What is the matter?"

"I almost shot you, Joe."

He paused a minute. "I'm glad you didn't."

"Me too."

Nothing more was said for a while. Joe never gave me instructions about quail shooting. I understood, however, that I should look for people first before looking for quail.

Later on that afternoon we came upon Joe's father finishing up some chore on his tractor. He called out to us, "How are you boys doing? Get any birds?"

"I've gotten a couple. Johnny's struck out so far." Nothing more was said about my almost shooting Joe that day.

On the Eastern Shore Sundays were God's days and shooting off sporting guns was frowned on. Joe had hung his birds outside the back door next to a bunch his father had shot the day before.

Early Sunday morning Mr. Valliant had plucked and cleaned the quail and Mrs. Valliant was baking them for lunch. What a meal!

We each had three birds which we slowly picked clean of meat and sucked the bones. They had a subtle wild flavor. There was squash and wild rice on the side.

I took the ferry back to Oxford that afternoon and walked to Jack's Point through the silent winter town. Mother and I closed up the house and drove back to Baltimore.

CHAPTER THIRTY-ONE

Years later with a young lady, Pat, I suggested that we spend the day exploring the Eastern Shore.

I picked her up early in the morning. We had lunch at the Tidewater Inn in Easton and walked the streets of the old quarter. I steered her past the old clapboard house which doubled as an auction and funeral business, then past the hospital to the Quaker Third Haven Meeting House. Pat was beguiled by these places.

After that we got back in the car and drove to Oxford. I drove her past our place at Jack's Point and then slowly drove through Oxford. We pulled the car up to the ferry dock below the now refurbished Robert Morris Inn and waited for the ferry over from Bellevue.

Pat and I walked out on the town dock which was attached to the ferry dock and watched the crabs and late summer sea nettles swim by the pilings. We watched the ferry pull in with its engine roaring. The Captain greeted us and said that Joe was away at college. I replied that I knew.

Pat and I stood at the rail and I pointed out Joe's place and the factory which had been his grandfather's. We drove through Royal Oak and past the Pasadena Inn and through St. Michael's. An auction was taking place at an old brick house. We joined the crowd and watched the bidding for a while, before leaving St. Michael's and returning to Baltimore.

CHAPTER THIRTY-TWO

A couple of years later, Joe called with the message that his mother had died.

A memorial service was scheduled at the little Methodist church in Royal Oak. Mrs. Valliant's second husband was a retired Episcopal minister, but the local Methodist minister had conducted the burial service for family at graveside.

I put on a dark suit and drove to the front of the little white shingled church. I walked around behind the building and opened the door, and found the ladies of the church busy at work in the kitchen. I saw trays of deviled eggs, ham and biscuits, dishes of celery, tiny cucumber sandwiches, and several large cakes. One of the ladies steered me through the kitchen out into the church, where I found a place in one of the pews off to the side.

The minister came out and stood in front of the raised altar and conducted a brief service. We all sang, "Oh, Mighty Father strong to save, whose arm hath bound the restless wave."

After the final prayer we were invited to the reception hall for "refreshments".

I went up to Joe and said a few consoling words. He introduced me to his stepfather, whom I had not met before. He was a short, stout man with a white, English-style mustache that matched his hair. He looked more like a retired major from the British army than a former Episcopalian minister.

I asked him how he was doing, not expecting anything out of the ordinary for an answer, but he replied, "I feel like I stepped off a cliff." A tear stood at the corner of his eye.

I felt very close to him. I had not expected to be let in.

CHAPTER THIRTY-THREE

Cove Hall was closed up for the last time.
New houses could not be built along Maryland's tide-water, but one could rebuild on old foundations. There had been a seventeenth-century brick house where Cove Hall stood, which had burned in the nineteenth century and been replaced with the frame house I had known. Maybe someday a seventeenth-century style brick house might rise on the spot again.

I would no longer sleep in the poster bed and look out long windows at the moonlight on the Tredavon and the twinkling lights of Oxford across the river as I dozed off. No longer would I stand leaning on the kitchen doorjamb. No more long talks on the screened porch or roaring laughter around the old dining table.

I love the Eastern Shore, and my childhood there.

$\mathcal{T}$*he author is available to speak on these subjects:*

- The Eastern Shore of Maryland as it was during his childhood days

- Antiques and Decorative Arts

- The author's experiences in antique hunting and selling

Please call him at
(410) 315-7940

APPRAISALS

John S. Pearson has been appraising antiques and decoratives arts for twenty years and his work is accepted by: museums, historic sites, insurance companies, law firms, courts, and agencies of the government.

Mr. Pearson appraises collections or individual items for insurance purposes, estates, gifts to institutions, and fair market value.

He may be reached by telephone at
(410) 315-7940

More Books from ℜecovery Communications, Inc.

ε⩒

Books available through your local bookstore

— and —
all authors are available for speaking and consulting nationwide

---

Diary of Abuse/Diary of Healing
by Jennifer J. Richardson, M.S.W.

Secret journal of a child, from age 6 til adulthood, recording two decades of physical and sexual abuse, with detailed healing therapy sessions. A very raw and extraordinary book.
Contact the author to speak at: (404) 373-1837

Turning Your Teen Around
How A Couple Helped Their Troubled Son
While Keeping Their Marriage Alive and Well

by Betsy Tice White

A doctor family's successful personal battle against teen-age drug use, with dozens of *powerfully* helpful tips for parents in pain. Describes the full gamut of emotions and healing of the entire family. Endorsed by John Palmer, NBC News.
Contact the author to speak at: (770) 590-7311

Getting Them Sober, Volume One

by Toby Rice Drews

Hundreds of ideas for sobriety and recovery. Endorsed by "Dear Abby" and Dr. Norman Vincent Peale.

Contact the author to speak at: (410) 243-8352

Getting Them Sober, Volume Four
Separation Decisions

by Toby Rice Drews

If you feel depressed because you can't leave; if you've left and gone back; much more.

Contact the author to speak at: (410) 243-8352

I See Myself Changing: A Meditation Journal

by Linda Meyer, Ph.D.

Wonderful weekly meditation book for all the teens/young adults in your life.

Contact the author to speak at: (217) 367-8821

Mountain Folk, Mountain Food
**Down-Home Wisdom, Plain Tales,
and Recipe Secrets from Appalachia**

by Betsy Tice White

The joy of living as expressed in charming vignettes and mouth-watering regional foods! Endorsed by the TV host of "Great Country Inns" and by *Blue Ridge Magazine*.

Contact the author to speak at: (770) 590-7311

Wise Stuff About Relationships

by Joseph L. Buccilli, Ph.D.

A *gem* of a book; "an empowering spiritual workout." Endorsed by the vice president of the *Philadelphia Inquirer*.

Contact the author to speak at: (609) 629-4441